World Heritage in Korea

World Heritage in Korea

Photographs by **SUH JAE-SIK**

HOLLYM

Elizabeth, NJ · Seoul

World Heritage in Korea

Copyright © 2001
by Suh Jae-sik

First published in 2001
Second printing, 2004
by Hollym International Corp.
18 Donald Place, Elizabeth, New Jersey 07208, USA
Phone: (908) 353-1655   Fax: (908) 353-0255
http://www.hollym.com

Published simultaneously in Korea
by Hollym Corporation; Publishers
13-13 Gwancheol-dong, Jongno-gu, Seoul 110-111, Korea
Phone: (02) 735-7551~4   Fax: (02) 730-5149, 8192
http://www.hollym.co.kr   e-mail: info@hollym.co.kr

ISBN: 1-56591-171-7
Library of Congress Catalog Card Number: 2001096204

Printed in Korea by Samsung Moonwha Printing Co., Ltd.
Phone: (02) 468-0361~5   Fax: (02) 461-6798

Bound in Korea by Myung Ji Mun Hwa Co., Ltd.
Phone: (02) 858-0101~9   Fax: (02) 858-0100

Contents

Preface

Korean cultural properties as a mirror of time attracts many world citizens. Korean cultural heritage calmly stands the abrasion of time and is not a simple accumulation of time, but a mirror of the Korean past, present and future.

Over time, the line, color, and shape of the Korean landscape has surpassed the regional limits of the Korean peninsula. World Cultural Heritage is a cultural property title designated by UNESCO. The committee of each country submits an application for registration of World Heritage status of their historical properties. The executive committee of UNESCO then deliberates and makes the final decision. The World Heritage Fund supports the World Heritage designation of cultural properties technically and financially. A World Cultural Heritage designation can upgrade a countries' cultural status. There are numerous World Heritage properties in Korea. They include Changdeokgung Palace, Hwaseong Fortress, Seokguram Grotto, Bulguksa Temple, Dolmen Sites, and Gyeongju Historic Area.

Underwater tomb of the Great King Munmu completed the unification of the Three Kingdoms

The history of Gyeongju is about the history of Silla. In B.C. 57, Silla was established in the Gyeongju area. This area is a good place to live because there are spacious and flat lands surrounded by mountains and rivers that flow in the middle of the land.

Gyeongju: City of Historic World Heritage Properties

The historic Gyeongju area contains numerous tombs, which are scattered throughout the city and remind us of very large hills. Many Silla's kings, queens and men and women of nobility lie beneath the tombs because Gyeongju was the capital city of Silla. Silla was the first united country of the Korean nation and there are traces of relics of Silla in Gyeongju. Gyeongju is surrounded by Mt. Namsan (it is also called Mt. Geumosan because it looks like a gold turtle looking toward at the East Sea). Mt. Sogeumsan in the north, Mt. Danseoksan in the west, Mt. Tohamsan in the east, and Mt. Myeong-hwalsan.

In the *Samguk Yusa* (Cultural Artifacts of the Three Kingdoms), there is a legend of the gold egg which tells about the founder of Silla. "The people of Silla went up to a high place and saw the southern part of their kingdom. At that time, an auspicious spirit descended beside a well. The people followed the spirit and found a gold egg before which a white horse knelt and bowed. Then the horse flew toward the sky. From within the egg a boy appeared, who was the founder of Silla." The well, which is located at the foot of Mt. Namsan, is called "Najeong Well."

The huge tombs are easily visible when you enter Gyeongju City. Ancient tombs form huge mounds which are called "Daereungwon (Place of huge tombs)." One of these tombs is 23m long by 120m wide. Among these tombs, Cheonmachong (Heavenly House Tomb) was excavated in 1973 at Gyeongju district. Many relics were found in this tomb. Among the 15,000 relics, there was a Cheomadojangni (Saddle flap with 'heavenly horse in the sky' painting). Eventually, the name of the tomb became "Cheonmachong."

Cheomseongdae (Astronomical Observatory) is about a hundred meters from "Daereungwon." It is an astronomical observatory which has a unique shape and looks like a bottle-shaped cylinder. The pedestal is square-shaped, the body is cylinder-shaped, and the Chinese character 井-shaped top is placed at the highest point of the structure.

Four angles of the 井-shaped top is points in four directions (east, west, north and south) respectively. It is 9.4 meters long and made of 365.5 rectangular stones. There are 365.5 days in a year in the lunar calendar.

Gyerim (Gyerim Forest) located near Cheomseongdae is the birthplace of Kim Alji, who was the legendary progenitor of the Gyeongju Kim clan, which has gained prestige as a sacred place of worship. The old twisted trees in this area have made the Gyerim all the more attractive, and the tomb of King Naemul is also here. Descendents of the Kim clan visit here everyday to worship.

Anabji Pond, which makes us aware of Silla's prosperity is 500 meters from Gyerim in the direction of Mt. Tohamsan. Anabji Pond was built in the 14th year of King Munmu (674) following the unified three kingdoms of Silla. In the middle of the huge pond, there are three islands and a mountain with twelve peaks, and it is said that it represents the Spirit of a legendary hermit with miraculous powers, one of the ancient Eastern thoughts. On the edge of the pond there are several buildings for feasts held on happy occasions.

Relics from Gyeongju historical area can be seen at the Gyeongju National Museum, especially the Geumgwan (Gold Crown) from the Geumgwanchong (Gold Crown Tomb) and Bogeom (Sword with gold inlay), from King Michu's tumulus. These treasures represent the Silla peoples' unique and elaborate artistic sense. In the outdoor exhibition hall, Seongdeokdaewangsinjong (Sacred bell of the Great King Seongdeok) is also a fantastic treasure which shows the splendid patterns and carving skills of the United Silla.

Bunhwangsa Temple is located at the side of Imhaero Road in front of Anabji Pond. Seokjeontap Pagoda (Stone pagoda) of Bunhwangsa Temple was built by piling stones that were trimmed into bricks. The pagoda is called the Seokjeon (stone-brick) pagoda.

Gyeongju, a gloriously prosperous city for 1,000 years, was the ancient capital city of Silla. Tile-roofed houses are clustered close together in Gyeongju city (above).

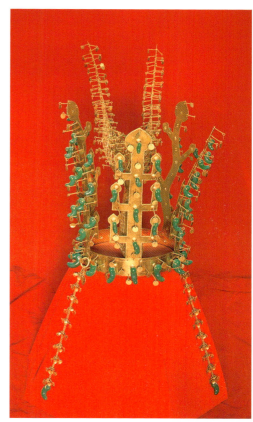

The smile of Silla (above) and The famous gold crown of Silla (above right). The front of the three-story stone pagoda at Gyeongju station (above left).

"Daereungwon (Royal tomb garden)" located in Hwangnam-dong is the old site of approximately 20 huge tombs. There are a mass of tombs between 10m and 120m in width and between 1m and 23m in length.

Cheonmachong (Heavenly Horse Tomb) where about 15,000 relics were excavated is presumed to be the tomb of the 22nd king of the Silla Kingdom. In this tomb, Cheonma-dojangni (Saddle flap with 'heavenly horse in the sky' painting) was excavated.

Anabji Pond was built in the 14th year of King Munmu (674) after Silla unified the three kingdoms. This pond shows the prosperity of the Silla period. In the middle of the huge pond, there are three islands and twelve mountain peaks, and it is said to represent the Spirit of a legendary hermit with miraculous powers, one of the ancient Eastern thoughts. On the edge of the pond there are several buildings for feasts held on happy occasions.

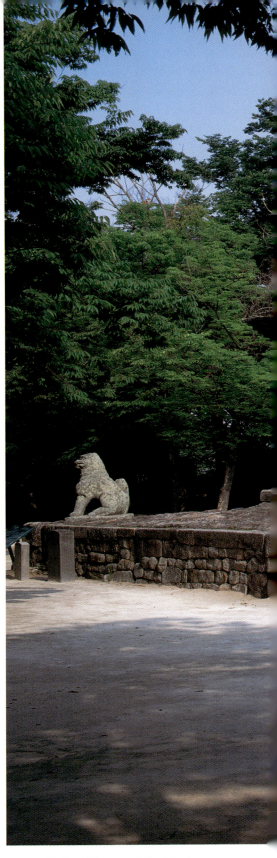

Seokjeon means stones piled and trimmed into bricks. The body of Seokjeontap Pagoda (Stone pagoda, National Treasure 30) of Bunhwangsa Temple, has four alcoves with stone gates on each face and Buddhist statues are placed in the four alcoves.

Both sides of each gate have a strong Inwangsang (a synonym of Geumgangyeksa, safeguard statue). The natural stone platform has a granite lion at each of the four corners.

Seongdeokdaewang Sinjong (Sacred bell of the Great King Seongdeok, National Treasure 29) is the largest bell existing in Korea. King Gyeongdeok of Silla (755) started casting the bell to honor the virtue of his father King Seongdeok, but he didn't see its completion. Later, it was completed by his son King Hyegong (771), and named Sacred Bell of King Seongdeok. This bronze bell is 3.33m high, 2.27m in rim diameter, and weighs about 25 tons.

 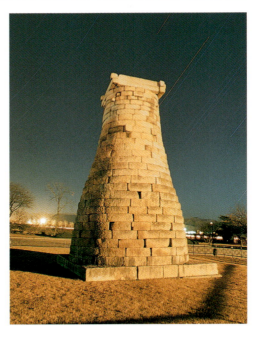

Cheomseongdae presumed to be the astronomical observatory of the Silla period has the most peculiar shape of all the Gyeongju relics. It is estimated to have been built in the period of Queen Seondeok (632 - 647). It is presently a little tilted to the northeast, but remains almost as it used to be. It is highly valued as the oldest astronomical observatory in Asia.

Hwangnyongsa Temple was started in the 14th year of King Jinheung (553) of the Silla Kingdom. To complete the construction of Hwangnyongsa Temple with its famous 9-story pagoda, it took 93 years. However, this great temple was burned during the Mongolian invasion in the 25th year of King Gojong (1238) of the Goryeo Kingdom. Now only the Hwangnyongsaji (Hwangnyongsa Temple site, Historic Site 6) remains.

Mt. Namsan in Gyeongju from the top of Mt. Tohamsan.

Chilburammaaeseokbul (Seated Buddha statue carved on rock surface near Chilburam Hermitage, Treasure 200) at Mt. Namsan in Gyeongju. The hands are in the hangmain position, which means 'to make evil surrender' and it is in the same posture as the principal statue at Seokguram Temple.

This large 2.7m-high Buddhist statue was presumed to be built during the eighth century, the Unified Silla period.

Maaeyeoraejwasang (Rock-carved seated Buddhist statue, National Treasure 201) and Tapgol-maaejosanggun (Rock-carved features at Tapgol village) in Bukji-ri, Bonghwa area. The statue is 9m high. Amita and Gwaneum on the western side present the Buddhist Elysium, Bosaengyeorae on the northern side presents the world of jubilation.

This statue is the oldest among the stone Buddhist images of Silla and was made at the close of the Silla period. It is located in an alcove and looks serene (far right). Namsanirwon (general area of Mt. Namsan, Historic Site 311) in Gyeongju.

Poseokjeongji (Poseokjeong pond site, Historic Site 1) in Gyeongju. Poseokjeong served as the pleasure spot of many Silla kings. They floated wine cups and chanted poetry around the abalone-shaped water canal (above and left).

Gyerim (Gyerim Forest, Historic Site 19) in Gyeongju is a prestigious site as the birthplace of Kim Alji, legendary progenitor of the Gyeongju Kim clan (below).

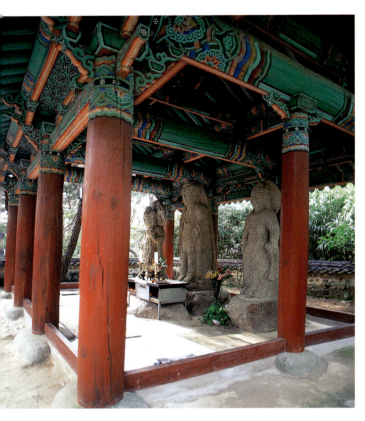

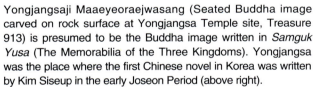

Yongjangsaji Maaeyeoraejwasang (Seated Buddha image carved on rock surface at Yongjangsa Temple site, Treasure 913) is presumed to be the Buddha image written in *Samguk Yusa* (The Memorabilia of the Three Kingdoms). Yongjangsa was the place where the first Chinese novel in Korea was written by Kim Siseup in the early Joseon Period (above right).

Anyone who sees the innocent smile of Baedong-samcheseokbul (Stone Buddha statue in Baedong) can escape the anguish of the mundane world (above).

Mt. Namsan in Gyeongju is designated as an historic site. Mireukgokseokbuljwasang (Seated stone Buddha statue at Mireuk Valley, Treasure 136), Yongjangsagok Samcheung-seoktap (Three storied stone pagoda at Yongjangsa Valley, Treasure 186), Yongjangsagok Seokbuljwasang (Seated stone Buddha at Yongjangsa Valley, Treasure 187), Bulgokseokbul-jwasang (Seated stone Buddha at Bulgok valley, Treasure 198), Sinseonam Maaebosalbangasang (Rock-cut seated bodhisattva near Sinseonam Hermitage, Treasure 199) and many other treasures are located in this area.

The elegant Samneung Valley surrounded by pine groves (left). Seochulji (Seochulji Lake, Historic Site 138) located at the foot of Mt. Namsan with lotus flowers and zinnia looks like a floating flower garden (above).

Gameunsa Temple in Gyeongju was built by King Munmu who wished to be buried in the East Sea and be reincarnated as a dragon to protect the nation. Now Gameunsaji (Gameunsa Temple site, Historic Site 31) remains (right). Jeonghyesaji Sipsamcheungseoktap (Thirteen storied stone pagoda, National Treasure 40)(above top).
Samcheungseoktap (Three storied stone pagoda, National Treasure 112)(above).

Seokguram Grotto, Bulguksa Temple : Buddha's Nation in a Mundane World

Bulguksa Temple is located at the foot of Mt. Tohamsan in Gyeongju. This temple was founded by Kim Daeseong in the 10th year of King Gyeongdeok (751) in the Silla period. It is said to be the earthly Buddhist Elysium of the past, present and future. It represents the spiritual world of the people of Silla.

The temple stands on the western mid-slope of Mt. Tohamsan overlooking the mythical mountain. Cheongun-gyo and Baegungyo (Cheongungyo and Baegungyo bridges, National Treasure 23) are connected to Bulguksa Temple. Both bridges have 33 steps respectively. They are representative of Korean stone bridges with their typical structure and beauty. The 45 degree angle of the steps is designed for climbing comfort.

There are two stone pagodas on the ground in front of Daeungjeon Hall as you go up the stairs. Dabotap Pagoda (Pagoda of many treasures, National Treasure 20) is about 10m high. With 261 stones, this pagoda is one of the masterpieces of the Silla period. Seokgatap Pagoda (Sakyamuni pagoda, National Treasure 21) is also representative of the beautifully constructed stone pagodas of Silla even though there are no decorations.

Bulguksa Temple is an amazing wondrous structure. It represents Buddha's deep meaning of truth and symbolizes Buddha's world. The wooden structures were burned during the war but the stone structures were preserved, and we can feel the warm touch of Silla's masons.

On the top of Mt. Tohamsan, there is a large granite Buddha in the Seokguram Grotto. This Buddha symbolizes Silla's Buddhist beliefs as a guardian god. It represents the 'essence of art' that contains the mystery of Silla.

Seokguram Grotto was also designed by Kim Daeseong in the same year as the construction of Bulguksa Temple. This grotto, in all its originality, displays the superiority of design of Seokguram Grotto.

The name of the temple was originally Seokbulsa which means a temple made of granite. But it is different from the temples of China and India in that it was made from piled stones. With its typical character, building skill, and superiority of design of the Buddha statue, Seokguram Grotto was designated a World Heritage property.

Seokguram Grotto is divided into Jeonsil (antechamber), Bido (corridor) and Husil (main rotunda). The main Buddha is seen from the antechamber. There are four guardian deities on the right and left sides respectively, eight in total. On the way to the main rotunda, there are four heavenly kings on the wall of the corridor. In the main rotunda, there is the main Buddha in the middle of the rotunda and ten disciples along the wall. There is also a Sipilmyeon Gwaneumbosal (Eleven-faced Avalokitesvara) behind the main Buddha and other Bodhisattvas.

The Silla people, along with the harmony of Buddhism, built the exquisite Bulguksa Temple and Seokguram Grotto.

Seokguram Grotto in Gyeongju contains the mystery of Silla and shows the beauty of Silla art. Seokbul (Buddha statue) at Seokguram with a benevolent face appears to show warmth even though it is made of stone.

Cheongungyo and Baegungyo (Cheongungyo and Baegungyo bridges, National Treasure 23) of Bulguksa Temple lead to the hall of Sakyamuni.

They are the most representative of stone bridges in Korea. The height and the angle of the steps were designed for climbing comfort.

Dabotap Pagoda (Pagoda of many Treasures, National Treasure 20), and Seokgatap Pagoda (Sakyamuni pagoda, National Treasure 21) of Bulguksa Temple. The two pagodas stand facing each other.
Dabotap shows the fine workmanship of Silla's masons and Seokgatap is beautifully well-balanced.

Bulguksa Temple symbolizes the serene world of Buddha in a mundane world. Namely, it means the world of hope and release from the suffering of life. In Bulguksa temple, there are spaces that symbolize this world, the next, and the previous world.

A drum for Buddhist rites, a wooden fish, a cloud-shaped bronze flat board, and a bell at the Buddhist temple are four objects in use at Buddhist temples. They are all sounders and are used at a rite offered before a statue of Buddha in the mornings and evenings.

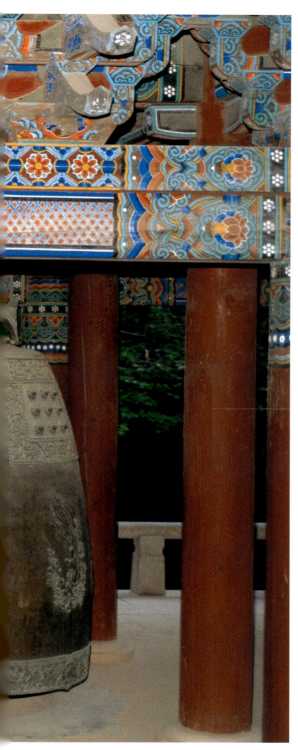

Daeungjeon rebuilt in 1765 is the main worship hall enshrining a gilt-bronze Buddha trio. The ground level stone and foundation stone of the Silla period still remains.
Especially the head of the dragon and phoenix sculptures show the aesthetics of the Silla structures.

Seokguram Grotto was founded by Kim Daeseong' in the 10th year of King Gyeongdeok (751) in the Silla Period. The original name was Seokbulsa, which means made of granite. The principal Buddha image, full of the power of life (left above), and Iljumun Gate at Seokguram Grotto (left below), The front room contains the principal Buddha image (above).

There are ten large stones that form the wall of the Grotto of the back room. The principal Buddha is placed slightly off the center and toward the back of the main chamber. From the entrance, the walls of the chamber are filled with the images of two heavenly gentlemen, two Bodhisattva and ten Arahats. Standing behind the principal Buddha is a statue of the eleven-faced Goddess of Mercy, perhaps the most exquisitely carved statue found inside the Grotto. A side section view of Seokguram Grotto (right above), A cross section of Seokguram Grotto (right).

There are statues of four heavenly guards on both the left and right sides of the front chamber, which is similar to the entrance to the Grotto. Carved on both sides of the entrance to the corridor is a statue of a heavenly guard. The narrow corridor is decorated with the four heavenly kings carved in pairs.

The serene appearance of the principal Buddha enshrined in the main chamber adds to the depth of the mystical atmosphere. The lines of the palm and foot, and fingernails are elaborately carved.

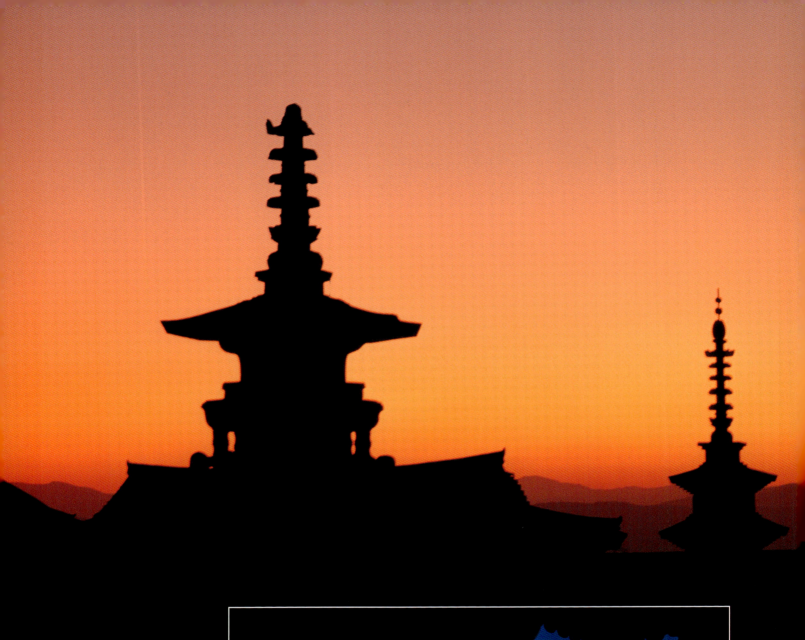

A view of the Dabotap Pagoda and Seokgatap Pagoda and a night view of Bulguksa on Buddha's birthday.

Tripitaka Koreana at Haeinsa Temple : The Symbol of Defender of the Fatherland

Every famous mountain in Korea has famous temples, and one of the most famous temples, Haeinsa Temple lies at Mt. Gayasan. Haeinsa Temple is one of the three famous Buddhist temples in Korea and symbolizes Buddhism as the defender of the fatherland. Because the temple houses the Tripitaka Koreana, it is widely known as Goryeo Daejanggyeong (Great Collection of Scriptures in Goryeo), or as Palman Daejanggyeong (Great Collection of Scriptures of Eighty Thousand Blocks) from the number of wood blocks containing the scriptures.

The Tripitaka Koreana at Haeinsa Temple are famous for their accuracy as well as their beautiful style of writing. Each wood block measures from 68 to 78cm wide, 24cm long and the thickness of the wood blocks vary from 2.6 to 4cm, weighing around 2,600 to 3,800 grams.

The excellent condition of the printing blocks of the Tripitaka Koreana has emerged as a challenge to modern preservation science. The timber was soaked in the sea for about three years and boiled in salt water in order to prevent decay and insect damage. They were then dried in the shade and lacquered after calligraphy engraving to prevent them from become warped. However, the manufacturing technology alone would not have been sufficient to preserve the numerous wooden blocks in such a perfect state over the centuries.

Janggyeongpanjeon (Storage halls for the Tripitaka Koreana woodblocks, National Treasure 52) is the wooden depository. It is located 1,430 meters above sea level on the south-western midslope of Mt. Gayasan.

Two buildings with 15 rooms in the front and 2 rooms in the side are placed side by side. Janggyeongpanjeon avoids much of decorations so that it could function only as the storage to preserve the Tripitaka.

For the ventilation and humidity levels and preservation of Tripitaka Koreana, it was built solidly and scientifically. To help control temperature and humidity, the site of Janggyeongpanjeon was leveled with charcoal, calcium oxide and clay. To maximize the ventilation, the storage halls have open grill windows. The front window is large and located on the upper wall and the back window is small and located on the lower wall. So the air is circulated in the hall naturally. All the natural and technical factors were considered.

Its scientific and rational design with a due consideration of nature enables the Tripitaka Koreana to be well preserved and recognized. Janggyeongpanjeon, built during in the 15 century, is the only place to preserve Tripitaka in the world.

Haeinsa Temple enshrines Daejanggyeongpan (Tripitaka Koreana (81,258 printing blocks), National Treasure 32) which is the symbol of the defender of the fatherland. It was built in the 3rd year of King Aejang (802) and is referred to as one of the three big temples of Korea.

Haein means the everlasting world of truth. This word derived from the Buddhist scriptures which contains the wisdom of Buddha.

The Daejeokgwangjeon (Hall of Immeasurable Light, Tangible Cultural Properties 256) at Haeinsa Temple (left below). Tripitaka Koreana are kept in Janggyeongpanjeon Hall at Haeinsa Temple. Among the many buildings in Haeinsa Temple, it was the only wooden building that maintained its old form and shape without damage during the Japanese invasion of Joseon because it was located deep in the mountain (far left).

The entrance of Janggyeongpanjeon Hall seen from the Sudarajang
(the Hall of Sutras). The eaves tiles
at twilight makes the lotus flower-
shaped shadow.

Started in the 24th year (1236) and finished in the 35th year of King Gojong of the Goryeo Kingdom (1251), Tripitaka Koreana is one of the most prized cultural treasures in Korea. Inside Janggyeongpanjeon.

樂果
禮樂
果天
地
之
和

般若波羅蜜多心經 唐三藏

觀自在菩薩行深般若
波羅蜜多時照見五蘊皆空度一切苦
厄舍利子色不異空空不異色色即
是空空即是色受想行識亦復如是舍
利子是諸法空相不生不滅不垢不淨
不增不減是故空中無色無受想行
識無眼耳鼻舌身意無色聲香味觸法
無眼界乃至無意識界無無明亦無無
明盡乃至無老死亦無老死盡無苦集
滅道無智亦無得以無所得故菩提
薩埵依般若波羅蜜多故心無罣
礙無罣礙故無有恐怖遠離顛倒夢
想究竟涅槃三世諸佛依般若波羅
蜜多故得阿耨多羅三藐三菩提故

The number of wood blocks is 81,340. They were engraved on both sides so the total number of blocks is 162,680. If they were printed and bound into books, there would be 6,815 volumes.

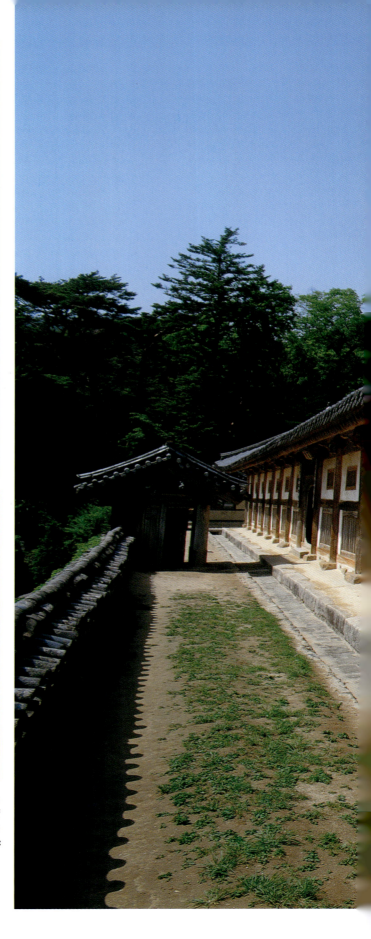

Janggyeongpanjeon Hall designed scientifically and rationally due to the consideration of preservation of Tripitaka Koreana. For the ventilation, the size of windows in the northern building called Beopbojeon (the Hall of Dharma) and the southern building called Sudarajang are different. It is an extremely scientific ventilation system.

In Haeinsa Temple, Buddhists line up, pass through Janggyeongpanjeon Hall and cross the front court of Gugwangru. They pray for the charity of Buddha and salvation of the people.

Mt. Gayasan in Hapcheon is home to one of Korea's three major Buddhist temples, Haeinsa Temple.

Hwaseong Fortress in Suwon: Apex of Scientific Structural Skill and Knowledge

King Jeongjo built Hwaseong (Brilliant Fortress) in memory of his late father. Hwaseong Fortress was constructed over a two and a half year period, and was designed by Jeong Yak-yong. It contains the magnitude of the East and the beauty of the West and is an apex of the scientific structural skills of Korea.

When King Jeongjo succeeded his grandfather, King Yeongjo, he ordered his father's tomb be moved from Mt. Baebongsan in Yangju, the eastern suburbs of Seoul, to Mt. Hwasan in Suwon.

The total length of the fortress was 5,418m and had 48 facilities originally, but it had been devastated in the war and suffered invasions for 200 years. It was restored at the end of 1970s.

For this construction, the crane was used for the first time in Korea and it created a standard for building construction sites. Hwapo Artillery was used as a defensive weapon, as well as scientifically made guns and bows.

The basic notion of Hwaseong Fortress was to renovate the existing fortress system. At that time the previous existing city was located on the plain and there were fortresses in the mountains. In two different defense systems, people usually lived on the plain but went to the fortress when they entered into a state of war. During those times, the village was usually devastated after a war whether they won the battle or not. To overcome these kinds of weaknesses, Hwaseong Fortress was strongly built.

Jeong Yak-yong, a young intellectual, who would later lead the school of Silhak (Pragmatic Studies) wrote about politics, economics, sociology, culture, as well as the arts and architecture. King Jeongjo commissioned him to design the fortress and plan its construction. He employed his scientific knowledge broadly, and one year later submitted his plan on the construction of the fortress.

King Jeongjo apparently planned to turn Suwon into a prosperous city by boosting commercial and manufacturing activities. And, as many historians assume, he probably dreamed of moving the capital there to be near the tomb of his beloved father and to carry out political reform away from the faction-minded courtiers in the capital.

The fortress originally had three observation towers named Gongsimdon Tower (meaning "Tower with empty interior"), one to the northwest, one to the south and one to the northeast. These towers were defensive facilities and were well constructed.

Usually every fortress had Ammun Gates (Gates for secret passage) built into the recesses of the fort in order to carry in food and arms without the enemy knowing. As for Hwaseong Fortress, there were three Ammun Gates such as the Seonam Ammun (South West Ammun Gate), Seo Ammun (West Ammun Gate), and Dong Ammun (East Ammun Gate). Seo Ammun was especially hard to find both inside and outside of the fortress.

In the eastern part of the fortress, there is the Bongdon Facility for communication and other walls for protection. Hwaseong Fortress in Suwon was a typical defensive fortress and a perfect military installation. Suwon city was built to display King Jeongjo's filial piety. That's why Suwon city is called a city of fortresses or a city of filial piety. Hwaseong Fortress is still a comfortable shelter as it was in ancient times.

Hwaseong Fortress in Suwon often referred to as the 'apex of Korean structural skill and knowledge' was built in the 18th year of King Jeongjo in the Joseon period (1794).

Banhwasuryujeong Pavilion represents the beauty of Hwaseong Fortress. It shows the subtle beauty of the structure and harmonizes well with the Yongyeon Pond.

Janganmun Gate located in the north is the main gate of Hwaseong Fortress and a representative structure of the fortress with the Paldalmun Gate (midday and night, right). Janganmun Gate is similar to Paldalmun Gate in shape and scale.

Hwahongmun Gate was established with seven stone floodgates. Among the seven sluices, the middle one is bigger than the others so clean water flows through the floodgate.

The spray of the water makes the Hwahongmun Gate look more beautiful. It is one of the eight beautiful sites in Suwon.

Dongbukgongsimdon built as a soldiers' training camp is located in the northeast corner of Hwaseong Fortress. Its oval shape makes it one of the peculiar looking buildings in the fortress. The height of Gongsimdon is 6.8m and there are spiral steps inside the structure.

The supervisional head office of Hwaseong Fortress was the Seojangdae Fort located on top of Mt. Paldalsan. From this fort you can get a view of the whole city and the fort's location made it easy to command soldiers.

Dongjangdae Fort (also called Yeonmudae Fort), was a command training fort (above), You can see the four directions at a glance, since there are no walls.
Changryongmun Gate (above left), Seonamammun Gate built into the recesses of the fort as concealed passages (left), Dongnamgakru Pavilion (far left).

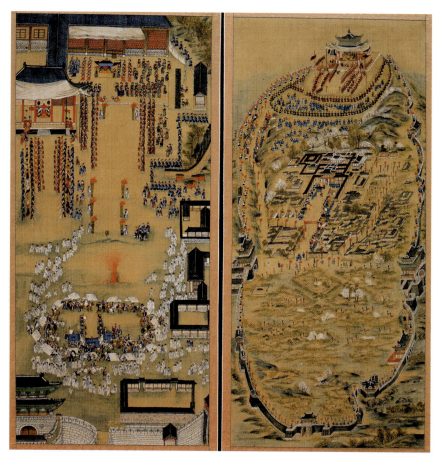

Parade in honor of Great King Jeongjo (above).
Hwaseong Fortress was built to follow the contour and height of the mountain, so it enclosed the valley with its mountain ridges. This Fortress was made of stones, earth, and bricks (left above and below).

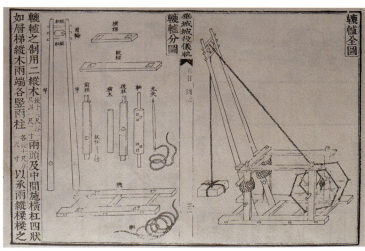

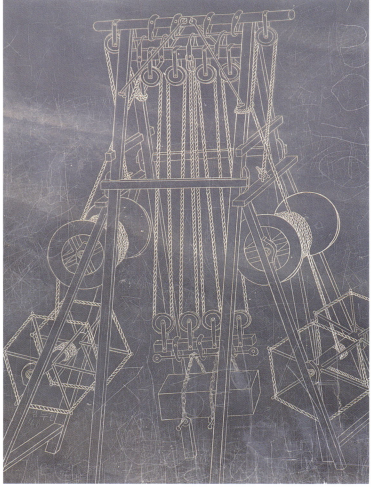

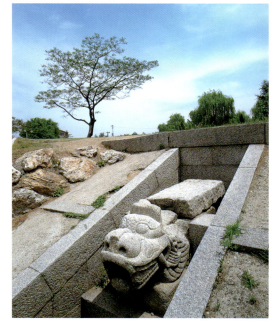

Bongdon used as a communication facility (above left). It communicated with Yukbong of Mt. Seokseongsan by signal fire and with Haebong of Hongcheondae Fort at sea. The first Geojunggi Crane in Korea (above) operated well.

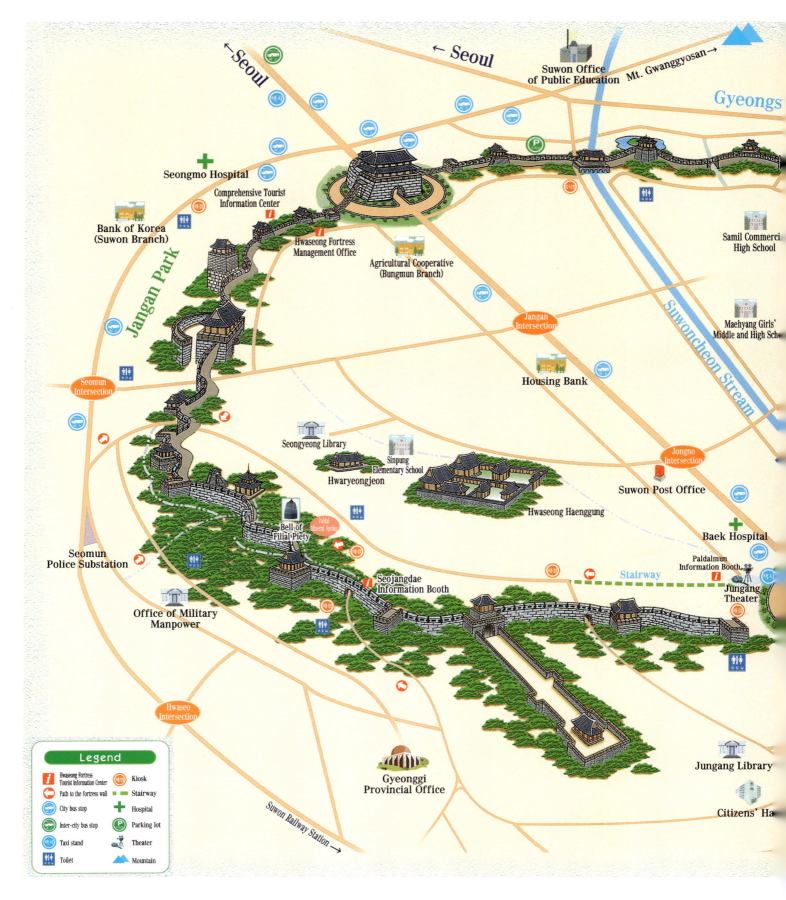

← Seoul

← Seoul

Suwon Office
of Public Education Mt. Gwanggyosan →

Gyeongs

Seongmo Hospital

Comprehensive Tourist
Information Center

Bank of Korea
(Suwon Branch)

Jangan Park

Hwaseong Fortress
Management Office

Agricultural Cooperative
(Bungmun Branch)

Samil Commerci
High School

Maehyang Girls'
Middle and High Sch

Jangan
Intersection

Housing Bank

Suwoncheon Stream

Seomun
Intersection

Seongyeong Library

Sinpung
Elementary School

Hwaryeongjeon

Hwaseong Haenggung

Jongno
Intersection

Suwon Post Office

Baek Hospital

Bell of
Filial Piety

Paldal
Mineral Spring

Seomun
Police Substation

Seojangdae
Information Booth

Paldalmun
Information Booth

Stairway

Jungang
Theater

Office of Military
Manpower

Hwaseo
Intersection

Gyeonggi
Provincial Office

Jungang Library

Citizens' Ha

Suwon Railway Station →

Legend

i	Hwaseong Fortress Tourist Information Center	예정	Kiosk
←	Path to the fortress wall	- - -	Stairway
🚌	City bus stop	+	Hospital
🚌	Inter-city bus stop	P	Parking lot
택시	Taxi stand	📷	Theater
🚻	Toilet	🔺	Mountain

96

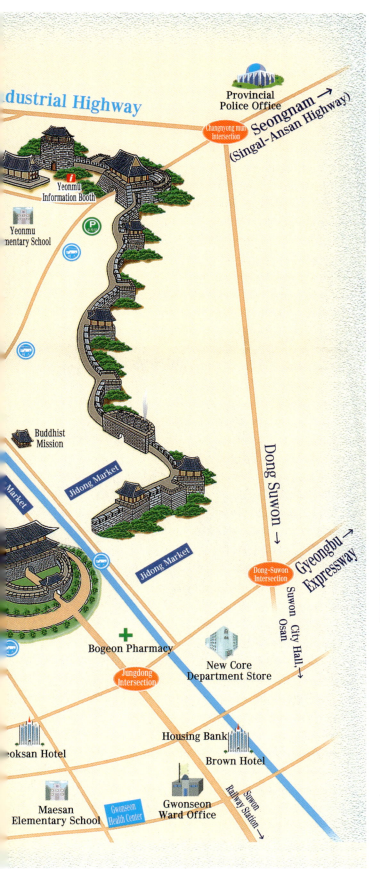

As for the scale of Hwaseong Fortress, the girth of the fortress is 5.7km and the area is 130ha. The eastern side of the fortress forms a low hill and the western side is in the shape of a castle. The tourists map published by the superintendent's office (left), Banghwasuryujeong Pavilion shows its beauty in all seasons (above).

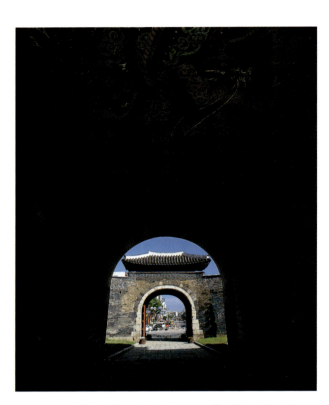

From Banghwasuryujeong Pavilion you can see the surrounding beauty of the scenery. It was made of stones, bricks, and timber and had the typical style architecture. With the elegant beauty of this pavilion in the moonlight, it is regarded as the first of the eight beautiful sites in Suwon.

Changdeokgung Palace : The Beauty of Joseon Dynasty

One of the buildings that shows wonderful harmony with nature, Changdeokgung Palace, is located in the middle of the capital city, Seoul. The meaning of Changdeok Palace is the palace of Prospering Virtue. It is also called the "East Palace" because it was located east of Gyeongbokgung Palace. It was built during the reign of King Taejong in Joseon Dynasty (1395-1910) and covers a total area of 580,000 square meters, except for the Secret Gardens. The Secret Gardens alone covers an area of 120,000 square meters.

If you pass through the Donhwamun Gate, the main gate of Changdeokgung, you can see Injeongjeon Hall and Daejojeon Hall first and then Biwon, the Secret Garden on the left, and Nakseonjae Hall on the right.

The secret garden is well-known as a representative palace garden in Korea. It has kept the landscape of the Joseon period and shows Korea's traditional natural landscape design. The back garden behind the inner hall where a luxuriant forest, lake and various sized pavilions were built, was considered an excellent example of Korea's traditional natural landscape design. The whispering of the wind in the trees, the songs of birds, and the sound of streams reverberate.

The small but lightly constructed Buyongji Pavilion was built on the shore of the Buyongji Lake. On the opposite side of the pavilion, Juhapnu Pavilion, where kings and scholars discussed their studies, stands high. There is also the Yeonghwadang Cottage, a noted place in the Secret Garden, and a place used for the civil service examination.

Through the Bullomun Gate (a gate of eternal youth) you can see the 99 kan (Kan means the unit of counting rooms) house. This cottage was built in 1828 according to the building style of a commoner's house.

Nongsujeong Pavilion is regarded as the most beautiful place of the many buildings in Yeongyeongdang Cottage. Nongsujeong literally means a pavilion located in the beautiful forest which has a simple but fascinating shape.

Along the path in the forest, you can see the Korean peninsula-shaped Bandoji Lake, the typical fan-shaped Gwanramjeong Pavilion, the Seungjaejeong Pavilion between the trees, and the small Banwolji Pond. In the surrounding area of Bandoji Lake, there are several buildings used as the library in the thick forest of pine trees, black oak trees, and maple trees. And then you arrive at Oknyucheon Stream made in the reign of King Injo (1636). There are five pavilions, and Cheongeuijeong Pavilion is one of them. "Choengeui" means blue rippling waves, so this pavilion creates a tranquil and serene atmosphere.

The Secret Garden was a place for the kings' rest and study. When the kings wanted to be alone and to get away from complicated politics, he visited this place of nature and beauty.

Nakseonjae Hall was made delicately and elaborately from the splendid flower wall to the foundation stones. In the huge flower bed of the Nakseonjae Hall to Sugangjae Hall, various flowers of the season were planted. Nakseonjae, Hall which is harmonious with nature, is estimated to be the most magnificent Korean building of the Joseon Dynasty. That's one of the reasons that Changdeokgung Palace and the Secret Garden were designated as World Heritage properties by UNESCO.

One of the representative buildings of Korea, Changdeokgung Palace, shows its perfect harmony with nature. Many other important buildings still remain.

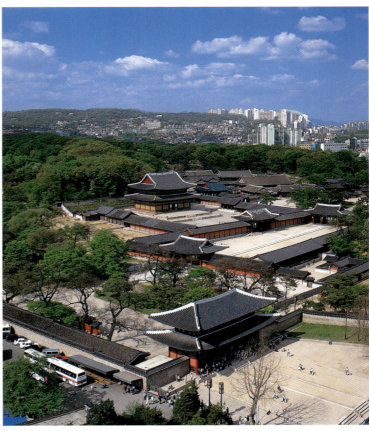

Entering into the main Donhwamun Gate, you can see the Injeongjeon Hall (left) served for official state functions, Daejojeon Hall and Nakseonjae Hall in Changdeokgung Palace. The original buildings were destroyed on several occasions, and during the Japanese Occupation the existing quarters became somewhat westernized.

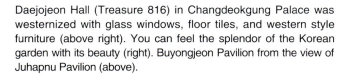

Daejojeon Hall (Treasure 816) in Changdeokgung Palace was westernized with glass windows, floor tiles, and western style furniture (above right). You can feel the splendor of the Korean garden with its beauty (right). Buyongjeon Pavilion from the view of Juhapnu Pavilion (above).

Inside Changdeokgung Palace, is remote from the noisy complexity of the capital city. Cool winds and the sound of flowing water adds to the calmness of the palace.

When the king wanted to gain high ranking officials' experience first hand, he wore the same attire and came to Yeongyeongdang Cottage. We realize that he also wanted to live as a commoner (above). Fan-shaped Gwallamjeong Pavilion (right).

The backyard of Changdeokgung Palace is beautiful in all four seasons.
Especially it is noted for the glorious colors of its autumn foliage which are harmonious with the eaves. The path in a small forest.

Two-story Juhapnu Pavilion built in the reign of King Jeongjo has great scenic beauty. The upper and lower stories were used as a banquet hall and a library respectively. The word "Juhap" means space-time, so it can be interpreted as a place for unofficial meetings.

Following the unfrequented path through the forest, where you can hear the birdcalls clearly, you can reach Oknyucheon Stream at the northern valley. The Spring water gushing from the bedrocks called Ojeong Well (the Kings well) is fresh and clear. Cheongeuijeong Building, which looks like a peaceful commoners house.

Inside Changdeokgung Palace and Nakseonjae where the concubines lived is more beautiful than before. From the gorgeous flower fences to the small cornerstones, everything is delicately constructed with wholehearted grace.

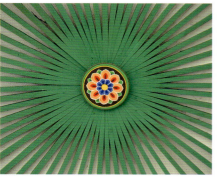

Moon-shaped Wolgwangmun Gate (above). The patterns of grapes, which means productivity and Japanese apricot flowers are elaborately carved (middle left). The figures of a mythical unicorn-lion and a turtle sit under the stone bridge (far left). Dancheong, the beautiful colored paintings (left).

Changing Guards Ceremony. The Geumgun Troops, directly responsible to the king, took charge of guarding the royal palace.

The troops which guard the gate of the palace change roles with the army which defends the outer walls of the palace. When the army arrives, the changing guards ceremony starts with the raising of the flag, musical instruments, and a command of drums.

Changdeokgung Palace covered with white snow. The court medical institution served both as a hospital and a pharmacy. Doctors and other medical staff members resided here. The hexagonal tall Sangryangjeon Pavilion located at the highest place in Nakseonjae Hall (far right). Euijingak Hall at Seunghwaru Pavilion lies between Changdeokgung Palace and Nakseonjae Hall (middle right).

Jongmyo Shrine: A Testimony to the Majesty of 500 Years of Joseon Dynasty

There are no colors, designs and splendid roofs but Jongmyo Shrine has the dignity and elegance that is beyond comparison anywhere in Korea. With 500 years of majesty of the Joseon Dynasty, Jongmyo Shrine is soaked with tranquility even though it is located in the middle of Seoul. Jongmyo Shrine was designated as a World Heritage property by UNESCO in December, 1995.

Jongmyo Shrine is the place where successive kings' tablets were preserved. Offering rites to ancestors was introduced to Korea in the Three Kingdoms Period from China. Jongmyo Shrine was erected in September, 1395 of the Joseon Dynasty (1392-1910) period, but most of the shrines were burned during the Japanese invasion of Korea in 1592. Many facilities that remain today in Seoul were rebuilt in 1608. The architectural structure of Jongmyo is not only simple but also dignified. It is one of the reasons that it is admired as a World Heritage property. There are two halls, Jeongjeon Hall (Main hall) and Yeongnyeongjeon Hall (Hall of eternal comfort). Jeongjeon Hall designated National Treasure 227 is the central building of Jongmyo and houses tablets of the Kings and Queens in 19 rooms. Yeongnyeongjeon Hall designated Treasure 821 houses all of the tablets which could not be housed in the main hall, and has 16 rooms. It is smaller than Jeongjeon Hall. The basic unit of the hall is the Sinsil Room. The entire hall is consists of each separate rooms for housing the tablets.

Moderate use of bright colors made the shrine moderate and dignified. The cloud patterned steps signify climbing to the heavens to see your ancestors. Korea still has the regular Jongmyojerye ceremony which is held on the first Sunday of May every year, in contrast to China which does not hold a similar ceremony. It has several procedures, such as greeting ancestors, enjoying a feast with ancestors and sending off ancestors.

Jongmyojerye (Jongmyo Royal Ancestral Memorial Ceremony, Important Intangible Cultural Property 56) includes music, songs, and dance. These elements are the requisite for the feast with wine and food from ancient times. Jongmyojeryeak (Jongmyo Royal Ancestral Confucian Memorial Ceremonial Music, Important Intangible Cultural Property 1), consists of performing with musical instruments, singing songs, and dancing.

For Jongmyojeryeak, pyeonjong (a bronze bell chime), pyeonggyeong (a jadeite chime), and many other musical instruments are used. Some instruments are performed on the terrace and others are played at the foot of the terrace. Two parts usually play the music by taking turns according to the procedure of the sacrificial rites.

Ilmu Dance performed at the Jongmyojerye varied according to the ancestor worshipped. That is, Parilmu (eight ilmu) for the king was performed by 64 people, Yugilmu (six ilmu) for the queen was done by 36 people. And Sailmu (four ilmu) for the high ranking officials was danced by 14 people. Jongmyojerye Rite, Jongmyojeryeak Music, and the Jongmyo Shrine are very precious and valuable to this day.

Jongmyojerye (Jongmyo Royal Ancestral Memorial Ceremony) is a ceremony held in the shrine for the kings and queens of the Joseon Period. Mr. Yi Gu is a descendant of the Joseon Dynasty and participated in the Jongmyojerye to pay respect to the ancestor's spirit.

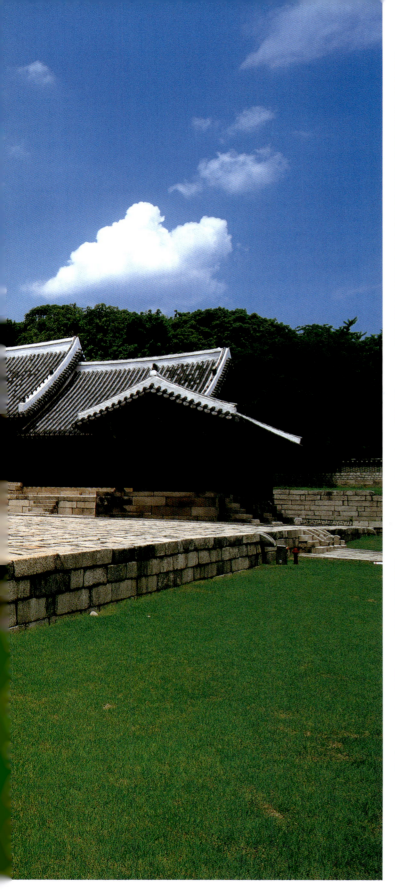

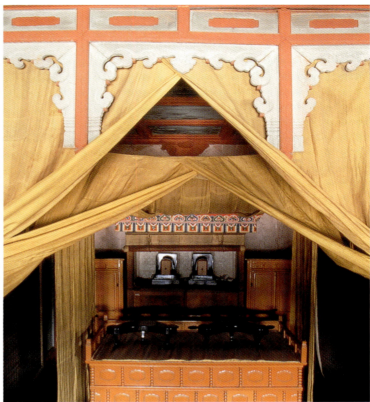

Jeongjeon Hall (Main hall of Jongmyo royal ancestral shrine) (left). There is a podium called "Woldae" for retainers' lining up in front of the King. These woldaes on the ground add to the Jongmyo Shrine's dignity. In the hall, each room was divided with blinds without any walls. Inside the room (above), there is Gamsil Shrine for consecration of an ancestral tablet, and space for the Jesa Rite for ancestors (far above).

Yeongnyeongjeon Hall (Treasure 821) was built as a separate shrine for enshrining all of the tablets that could not be housed in the main shrine, Jeongjeon Hall. It housed the tablets for the great-great-grandparents of King Taejo, founder of the Joseon dynasty.

Jongmyo Shrine was a place that enshrined the tablets for Kings and Queens of Joseon Dynasty and held the rites. Instead of the brightly decorated structure, it used subdued colors and patterns of architecture to dignify the shrine.

Regular Jongmyojerye ceremonies at Jeongjeon Hall and Yeongnyeongjeon Hall are held every year on the first Sunday of May. With the civil and military officers' parade on the road outside, this ceremony starts in the halls.

Among the Jeonju Yi's descendants, selected officiants at rites conduct the ceremony. According to the head officiant's lead, selected officiants wash their hands (right above), Offering wine to the tablet (far above), Officiants' enter (left).

pJongmyojerye has been held continuously since 1395 when the Joseon Dynasty (1392-1897) completed the State. Its order and procedures were very strict and solemn because it was a model of all ceremonies for the spirits.

Jongmyojeryeak (Jongmyo Royal Ancestral Confucian Memorial Ceremonial Music) was re-enacted by the Yi family of Jeonju and the National Center for Korean Traditional Performing Arts at Jeongjeon Hall in Jongmyo Shrine in 1988.

With 390 people, this large-scale performance took 2 hours and a half. For this event, about 5,000 spectators, including many foreign visitors, watched the performance.

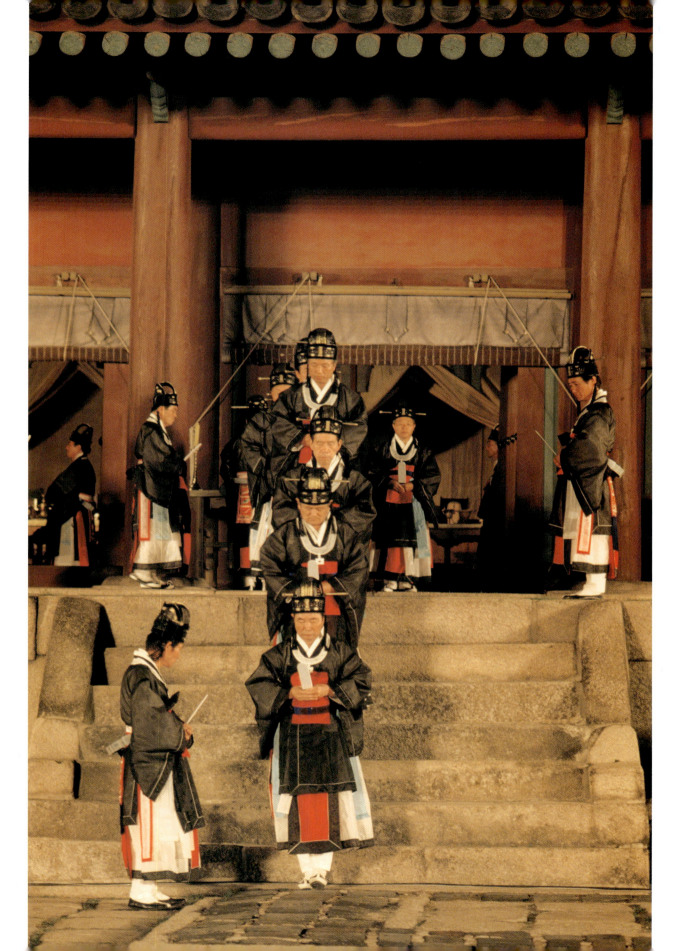

Vessels for memorial service of the deceased and sacrificial offerings. All sacrifices uncooked are offered to ancestors and vessels designated as cultural assets are used.

The Parilmu Dance is performed by 64 persons to the accompaniment of two orchestras playing classical Jongmyojeryeak Music with the sound of bell chimes. In the Munmu Dance (Civil officials' dance), performers hold the yak (a wind instrument) in the left hand and the danjeok made from the feathers of pheasants in the right hand. In the Mumu Dance (Military officers' dance), dancers hold a wooden spear and wooden sword.

For Jongmyojeryeak, pyeonjong (a bronze bell chime), pyeonggyeong (a jadeite chime), banghyang (metal chimes), jingo (a long barrel drum), janggu (a double-headed hourglass-shaped drum), ajaeng (a bowed zither), jeolgo (a medium-sized barrel drum), bak (a fan-shaped wooden clapper), haegeum (a two-string spike fiddle), daegeum (a large transverse bamboo flute) and other musical instruments are used.

Dolmen Sites: Area of Eternal and Immortal Spirit

Goindol Dolmen represents the cultural artifacts of prehistoric Korea. Dolmens are tombs which consist of a large rock and several smaller rocks supporting the larger rock.

These two words, Goindol Dolmen and Jiseongmyo Cromlech, usually have the same meaning, but Jiseongmyo means the tomb that Goindol dolmens scattered throughout Korea. People used the huge stones not only for building material but also for worshipping their mystical powers. This means that it was believed the huge stone had a spirit that governs people's fortune and misfortune. So Goindol Dolmen is precious in that it shows the Korean people's spirit.

At Jiseongmyogun Dolmens in Gochang (Historic Site 391), a total of 442 dolmens have been found which is the largest collection in the world. It includes the table-shaped style, the go-board-shaped style, and many other diverse shapes. It is estimated that the number of dolmens in Korea is over 60,000.

The Korean Goindol Dolmen is divided into three types, i.e., Southern style, Northern style and the Gaeseok style which consists of only one big ceiling stone (capstone style). Generally the Southern style is the go-board-shaped dolmen and was famous in the early Iron Age. This dolmen site was found south of Hangang River in Jeolla-do and Gyeongsang-do.

The Northern style is the table-shaped dolmen and is usually found north of Hangang River in the Pyeongannam-do and Hwanghae-do convergently. They are also found at mountainous areas in Gangwon-do. In the western coastal area, these dolmens stand on a hill in the Gochang-eup, Jeollabuk-do province.

As for the Gaeseok style dolmen, they have a nationwide distribution. So it is the representative style of Korean goindol dolmen. As compared with the numbers and scale of the goindol Dolmen, the burial artifacts are rare and are limited in number and kind. Among the burial accessories, the majority are arrowheads and stone swords. Besides stone axes, stone spinning machines, earthenware, and other jade ornaments were found.

The distribution of arrowheads have been found nationwide and stone swords were found at the house sites. Half moon-shaped stone swords were found around the Gaeseok style dolmen sites and stone axes with both-sided blades or round shaped were found around the Northern style dolmen sites.

Generally speaking, the goindol dolmen is referred to as tombs made with stones from the Bronze Age. These dolmens are distributed extensively in Europe in places such as France, the United Kingdom, Africa such as Ethiopia, the Republic of the Sudan, and India, Indonesia, China, and Japan.

In Korea, the dolmens which were made thousands of years ago are scattered all over the country including Jejudo Island, Heuksando Island and Ullengdo Island. Especially the Gochang, Hwasun, Ganghwa dolmen sites are famous for the large group of dolmens worldwide.

The prehistoric cemeteries at Gochang, Hwasun, and Ganghwa contain many hundreds of examples of dolmens and the highest density and greatest variety of dolmens in Korea. These areas were designated as World Heritage properties by UNESCO.

Jiseongmyo Cromlech at the Jidong village in Dosan-ri, Gochang-gun. The value of this dolmen is recognized because it figured prominently as a tomb system of the Bronze Age.

Hundreds of dolmens lie scattered in the Goindol valley in the Hwasun area, Jeollanam-do Province. Especially the larger rocks that weigh 200 tons were discovered and became the center of public attention. The Goindol Dolmen above was found in the vicinity.

Jiseongmyogun Dolmens in Gochang (Historic Site 391), a total of 442 dolmens have been found and are the largest in the world. They include the table-shaped style, the go-board-shaped style, and other diverse shapes. It is estimated that the number of dolmens in Korea is over 60,000.

The Northern style dolmen found at the southern part of Korea is located at the Jidong village in Dosan-ri, Gochang-gun (above). It was originally shaped like an oval (bottom left). Dolmen at Maesan village in Gochang (above left).

In Korea, the total number of dolmens is estimated to be over 60,000. Dolmens at the Jungdo park in Chuncheon, Gangwon-do (far above right). dolmen at Hyosan-ri, Hwasun-gun, Jeollanam-do (far above left). Dolmen on the tomb at Jungnim-ri, Gochang-gun, Jeollanam-do (above and left).

Goindol Dolmen park where preserved dolmens from Suncheon, Boseong, Hwasun areas and various historic relics of the Prehistoric Age (left) are on display.

Displaying the dolmens (bottom left). Stone sword, earthenware, and stone arrowheads were unearthed at the construction site of the rapid transit railway in Chilgok-gun, Gyeongsangbuk-do.

The biggest Jiseongmyo Cromlech in South Korea is 2.6m in height and 5.5m in width. The capstone of the dolmen is 7.1m in length and it is in the typical northern style.

About the author

Text and Photographs by Suh Jae-sik

SUH JAE-SIK is a well known photographer who has published widely and has won a number of prestigious awards both nationally and internationally. In 1986, he was a photographer/ reporter for the Asian Games, and again in 1988 for the Olympic Games. For his remarkable photography, he received the "Ministry of Culture and Tourism Prize" at the photography competition held under the auspices of the Korea National Tourism Organization. In addition, he has received more than 50 prizes at various photography competitions. He published "The Beauty of Korea" in 1998 and "The Beauty of Seoul" in 2001. In 1999, he was commissioned to work on the book, "Hanoak: Traditional Korean Homes." For this outstanding work, he received the "Hankuk Baeksang Publishing Culture Grand Prix" that was conferred by the Hankuk Ilbo Daily Newspaper.

  Mr. Suh had worked as a photographer for "Hanguk Hwabo" and the magazine "Seoul." Most recently, his photographs can be seen in "Sweet Place for Living," a magazine published by Goyang City. He was also the photographer of the internationally well-known book, "The Spirit of Korea Taekwondo." Currently he is working on "The Thirty-Year History of Pohang Steel." Mr. Suh, a member of the Korea Photographer's Association, is an outstanding photographer who has greatly influenced the field of photography in Korea.

(Telephone) 02-442-8084
(Cellular phone) 011-891-8088
(E-mail) sjaesik@hanmail.net